Bible reflections
for older people

The Bible Reading Fellowship
15 The Chambers, Vineyard
Abingdon OX14 3FE
brf.org.uk

The Bible Reading Fellowship (BRF) is a Registered Charity (233280)

ISBN 978 0 85746 591 7

Acknowledgements
Scripture quotations taken from The Holy Bible, New International Version (Anglicised edition) copyright © 1979, 1984, 2011 by Biblica. Used by permission of Hodder & Stoughton Publishers, a Hachette UK company. All rights reserved. 'NIV' is a registered trademark of Biblica. UK trademark number 1448790.

Scripture quotations from The New Revised Standard Version of the Bible, Anglicised edition, copyright © 1989, 1995 by the Division of Christian Education of the National Council of the Churches of Christ in the United States of America. Used by permission. All rights reserved.

Scripture quotations from the Good News Bible published by The Bible Societies/HarperCollins Publishers Ltd, UK © American Bible Society 1966, 1971, 1976, 1992, used with permission.

Scripture quotations from the Contemporary English Version. New Testament © American Bible Society 1991, 1992, 1995. Old Testament © American Bible Society 1995. Anglicisations © British & Foreign Bible Society 1996. Used by permission.

Every effort has been made to trace and contact copyright owners for material used in this resource. We apologise for any inadvertent omissions or errors, and would ask those concerned to contact us so that full acknowledgement can be made in the future.

A catalogue record for this book is available from the British Library

Printed and bound by CPI Group (UK) Ltd, Croydon CR0 4YY

Contents

About the writers

Jennifer Rees Larcombe is one of BRF's most popular writers. She has six children and 15 grandchildren. She loves her garden, but sometimes tears herself away to speak at conferences around the country. She still works as a counsellor as well as a writer, but most of all she enjoys being a grandmother.

Paul Harris is a poet, writer and broadcaster based in Bournemouth. His published work includes two poetry collections, and non-fiction works on spirituality, leadership and communication. He performs poetry at festivals and venues in the UK and abroad, and is currently co-writing a TV sitcom. He is married to Cathy, a speech therapist, and they have four sons and eight grandchildren.

Albert Jewell lives in Leeds and has been a Methodist minister for 55 years, serving in a succession of pastoral, ecumenical and educational positions. Since 'retiring', he has completed a PhD in ageing studies and is currently researching in the field of dementia. He and his wife Gill have two children and five grandchildren, and rejoice in the recent addition of a great-granddaughter.

Ro Willoughby has been writing and editing Christian resources for many years. She is currently a Licensed Lay Minister at St Michael's Highgate, where she is engaged in ministry with people of all ages, and regularly leads Barnabas in Schools RE Days. She loves creating food that looks and tastes good! No surprise that she also enjoys entertaining.

From the Editor

Welcome! We hope you enjoy this new collection of Bible reflections and find encouragement and inspiration in these pages.

Our writers are all very different, but each one of them brings fresh, intriguing insights, drawn from long years of experience and a deep knowledge of the Bible. **Jennifer Rees Larcombe** wanders around Capernaum watching Jesus meet his neighbours. **Paul Harris** writes of an exuberant, overflowing, ridiculous hope forged from pain and loss. **Albert Jewell** writes with sensitivity and understanding of the gift, and fragility, of memory, and **Ro Willoughby** begins her series on welcome and acceptance with a delightful story of her then four-year-old son solemnly offering to take visitors' coats and make them tea.

In the centre pages, **Debbie Thrower**, Team Leader of BRF's The Gift of Years ministry, meets fascinating, inspiring people like climate change activist **Christine Whild**, and introduces newly discovered poets like **Carla McCowen**, who has been writing all her adult life but has only recently released her work into the wild.

As you read these Bible reflections and spend time with God, we pray that you will know his presence, and know, as Ro Willoughby puts it so well, that 'God loves us so we love him. We come close to him, so he comes close to us.'

God bless you

Eley
x

Using these reflections

Perhaps you have always had a special daily time for reading the Bible and praying. But now, as you grow older, you are finding it more difficult to keep to a regular pattern or find it hard to concentrate. Or maybe you've never done this before. Whatever your situation, these Bible reflections aim to help you take a few moments to read God's word and pray, whenever you are able.

When to read them

You can read these Bible reflections in the morning or last thing at night, or any time during the day. Why not use them as a way of making 'an appointment to be with God'?

There are 40 daily Bible reflections, grouped around four themes. Each one includes some verses from the Bible, a reflection to help you in your own thinking about God and a suggestion for prayer. The reflections aren't dated, so it doesn't matter if you're not able to read them every day. The Bible verses are printed, but if you'd like to read from your own Bible, that's fine too.

How to read them

- **Take time** to quieten yourself, becoming aware of God's presence, asking him to speak to you through the Bible and the reflection.

- **Read** the Bible verses and the reflection:
  - What do you especially like or find helpful in these verses?
  - What might God be saying to you through this reading?
  - Is there something to pray about or thank God for?

- **Pray**. Each reflection includes a prayer suggestion. You might like to pray for yourself or take the opportunity to think about and pray for others.

The good neighbour

Jennifer Rees Larcombe

When someone new moved into our village, everyone was eager to know what they were like and if they would 'fit in'. This was particularly true of those of us who had lived there longest. I wonder how the people felt in the little fishing village of Capernaum, when Jesus arrived to make his home there. Perhaps they had already heard the gossip about how he had escaped from his home town of Nazareth. Everyone there had known him as their village carpenter, so when he stood up in the synagogue and said he was the Messiah, they were so infuriated they tried to kill him.

Perhaps some residents of Capernaum didn't like the idea of having a 'troublemaker' like that as a neighbour. They wouldn't have wanted to upset the Roman soldiers who were stationed in a fort on the outskirts of their village. Everyone thought that the Messiah, when he came, would drive out the Romans, so this crazy imposter might cause serious trouble in the district. So maybe, at first, some people eyed Jesus with hostility.

Yet, to other villagers, he became the best neighbour they ever had. Suppose we put ourselves into the shoes of some of the very different kinds of people who lived close to Jesus in Capernaum; we might discover that many of them were a lot like us.

John 1:41–42 (NIV)

First introductions

The first thing Andrew did was to find his brother Simon... And he brought him to Jesus. Jesus looked at him...

Four young fishermen from Capernaum, eager for adventure, took a few days off work to go and hear John the Baptist, the preacher everyone was talking about. 'Get your lives cleaned up because the Messiah's coming,' he thundered at the crowds. James, John and Andrew lapped it all up enthusiastically and, when John pointed to a man in the crowd and said, 'There's your Messiah,' they would have been wild with excitement.

But I suspect Simon felt uncomfortable. He knew only too well that his character matched his name – which meant 'wobbly reed'. He had always been rash, unreliable and easily led into trouble. Perhaps when his brother Andrew wanted to introduce him to Jesus, he felt he 'wasn't good enough'. How astonished he must have been when Jesus looked at him with such kindly eyes, even though he seemed to know everything about him, and said, 'I'm going to change your name from "Wobbly Reed" to "Rock Man"' – from Simon to Peter. Maybe Simon suddenly realised that Jesus was able to help him change into the kind of man he had always wanted to be. We are never too old for Jesus to change us.

■ **PRAYER**

Lord, you know how 'wobbly' I feel sometimes – worried about so many things. Give me the kind of rock-like courage you gave Peter. Amen

Mark 1:16, 19–20 (NIV)

Abandoned?

As Jesus walked beside the Sea of Galilee, he saw Simon and his brother Andrew… When he had gone a little farther, he saw James son of Zebedee and his brother John… He called them, and they left their father Zebedee in the boat with the hired men and followed him.

I've always wondered how Zebedee felt about being abandoned by his sons, James and John. Did he wonder how he would manage without them – and without his other partners, Simon and Andrew?

When two of my children moved abroad to serve the Lord, I felt lost. Somehow we expect our family members to be there for us when we get a bit older, but sometimes they're genuinely too busy or move too far away – just when we most need their help and support. I found it desperately hard letting go but, looking back now, I can see how their loss developed my faith in God's ability to meet my practical and emotional needs. Zebedee and his wife are so often mentioned later in the story that they obviously came to believe in Jesus too, and his wife even followed Jesus right to the cross (Matthew 27:56). Jesus has a way of disrupting our lives, but only because he longs for us to become ever more dependent on him.

■ PRAYER

Lord, I've lost so many people I used to depend on for help and guidance. Please help me to keep depending on you for every detail of my life. Amen

Mark 1:30–31 (NIV)

Mother-in-law

Simon's mother-in-law was in bed with a fever... So [Jesus] went to her, took her hand and helped her up. The fever left her.

Last Christmas Day, lots of my family were arriving when I collapsed into bed with raging flu. Listening to the chaos in the kitchen certainly didn't make me feel any better. So I definitely feel for Simon Peter's mother-in-law when he invited several unexpected guests for lunch. His impetuous character might not have made him an easy son-in-law. She must have felt so helpless. Perhaps she worried whether her daughter would manage to cook for so many.

Jesus could easily have healed her with one word from a distance, but instead he chose to go to her, take her hand and help her to get up. When we are 'getting on in years', tenderness and someone's undivided attention are among the things we can value most. When we are older and slower, ill, forgetful or in pain, we sometimes feel we're in the way and even a nuisance, but from today's story we can see how very differently Jesus feels towards us, and how much he cares for us.

■ **PRAYER**

Lord, I love the gentle way you care for me. You listen to everything I say, and you are constantly interested in everything I do. Help me treat others as you treat me. Amen

Luke 5:23–24 (NIV)

Tricky emotions

'Which is easier: to say, "Your sins are forgiven," or to say, "Get up and walk"? But I want you to know that the Son of Man has authority on earth to forgive sins.' So he said to the paralysed man, 'I tell you, get up, take your mat and go home.'

I wonder how the owner of the house would have felt when the roof was dramatically ripped open to allow the paralysed man to get to Jesus. When the man came down through the roof, most likely everyone expected to see another physical healing. Only Jesus knew that the man needed more than this; that he was also paralysed by regrets and was in need of forgiveness.

We don't know what he had done, but Jesus knew that he was crippled by shame as much as by physical helplessness, so he healed him by offering him forgiveness. Shame, fear and regret can trap us too, making us unable to do all sorts of things and sometimes damaging our relationships. As Christians, we believe Jesus both heals and forgives. We may not know how our physical and spiritual needs are related, but he does, and I firmly believe that just as we pray for healing in the face of illness, so too we can pray for help in overcoming our fears and 'if-onlys'. Which of your secret emotions do you need Jesus to heal?

■ **PRAYER**

Lord, please take authority over these feelings which make me feel so helpless. Amen

Matthew 8:3 (NIV)

Loneliness

Jesus reached out his hand and touched the man. 'I am willing,' he said. 'Be clean!'

He was the loneliest man in the village. No one had touched him for years. His family climbed the hill from Capernaum to leave him food on the hillside, but dared not come near enough to talk. From his cave, he could watch the busy harbour and bustling market, but he must have felt desperately isolated up there alone. Then one day crowds streamed up the hill and, from his hiding place, he could hear someone preaching. Was it the love behind the radical words of the Beatitudes that gave him courage to approach Jesus? I wish I'd been there the day he arrived home in Capernaum, cured.

Loneliness and isolation can haunt people of our age. Not only have I lost people I loved and who once shared my life, but health problems have sometimes cut me off from friends and activities. Nevertheless, I'm determined to keep remembering that Jesus calls me his friend (John 15:15) and values my companionship far more than the work I used to do for him.

■ PRAYER

Lord, I find it so easy to focus on all that I've lost rather than allowing my loving relationship with you to become my highest priority. Amen

Luke 5:27, 29–32 (NIV)

Regrets

After this, Jesus went out and saw a tax collector by the name of Levi sitting at his tax booth. 'Follow me,' Jesus said to him... Then Levi held a great banquet for Jesus... But the Pharisees and the teachers of the law who belonged to their sect complained to his disciples, 'Why do you eat and drink with tax collectors and sinners?' Jesus answered... 'I have not come to call the righteous, but sinners to repentance.'

As I look back over my life, I realise I made some bad mistakes. I wonder if Levi, later called Matthew, wished he'd never chosen to work for the Romans, cheating and robbing his neighbours until they hated him.

His tax office was on the quayside, so he may have heard Jesus preaching from Peter's boat, but perhaps that only made him feel worse about himself? Then one day there was Jesus smiling down at him, offering him friendship and the chance to change. He left his job with such joy in his heart that he invited all his dishonest and despised friends to dinner so he could introduce them to Jesus. How that party enraged his religious, self-righteous neighbours! I am so glad that Jesus came for people like us who make mistakes and need his forgiveness, often.

■ PRAYER

Lord, sometimes I shudder when I look back over my life, remembering some of the things I wish I'd never said or done. I know you've forgiven me, but please help me forgive myself. Amen

John 4:46, 49–50 (NIV)

The rich man

And there was a certain royal official whose son lay sick at Capernaum… The royal official said, 'Sir, come down before my child dies.' 'Go,' Jesus replied, 'your son will live.'

This nobleman probably lived in a luxurious villa above the village, but his vast wealth meant nothing when his boy lay dying. So he rode 20 miles in search of Jesus. Most people would have been flattered if the richest and most important man in the district asked for help. But, to everyone's astonishment, Jesus refused to go with him.

Jesus doesn't always answer our prayers as, or when, we want. All the rich man had to cling to, as he rode the long miles home, was Jesus' promise: 'Your son will live.' Perhaps he kept repeating that promise over and over. While I wait for God's response to my prayers, I find that repeating his promises really helps, and I try to remind myself that it is while we wait that our faith grows. How wonderful to read that the whole of the nobleman's household became followers of Jesus (John 4:53). Have you ever seen God answer prayers for your family in a remarkable way?

■ **PRAYER**

Lord, keep me from discouragement as I wait for you to answer my prayers. Amen

Mark 3:1–2, 5 (NIV)

Transformed

Jesus went into the synagogue, and a man with a shrivelled hand was there. Some of them were looking for a reason to accuse Jesus, so they watched him closely to see if he would heal him on the Sabbath… [Jesus] looked around at them in anger and, deeply distressed at their stubborn hearts, said to the man, 'Stretch out your hand.' He stretched it out, and his hand was completely restored.

Because the man's hand and arm were 'shrivelled', it probably meant he could not earn his own living. Without a welfare state, this might have made him and his family homeless beggars. Yet some of his heartless neighbours saw him only as bait to trap Jesus into breaking one of their petty religious rules. Jesus could see how much sadness and loss this man's disability had caused, but what deeply distressed him were the cold uncaring faces surrounding him. Why do we, who love God, so often criticise others? We disapprove of the Sunday sermon, complain about loud worship music and grumble about disruptive children. Does Jesus sometimes look sadly round our churches on Sundays?

I love this story because it shows how much Jesus understands the difficulties of disablement. At our stage in life, others don't always understand how strokes, falls and arthritis can rob us of so many good things. Jesus cared more about this man's problems than about his own reputation, and he cares about our problems too.

■ **PRAYER**

Lord, give me your kind of love. Amen

Luke 8:41–44, 48 (NIV)

Who is a VIP?

Jairus, a synagogue leader, came and fell at Jesus' feet, pleading with him to come to his house because his only daughter, a girl of about twelve, was dying. As Jesus was on his way, the crowds almost crushed him. And a woman was there who had been subject to bleeding for twelve years… [She] came up behind him and touched the edge of his cloak… He said to her, 'Daughter, your faith has healed you. Go in peace.'

Everyone honoured and looked up to Jairus because he led the synagogue. They would have been astounded to see him kneeling before Jesus. Jews refused to kneel to anyone but God (Esther 3:2–4). Most of the other local religious leaders rejected Jesus, but perhaps Jairus was beginning to believe he was the Messiah.

In contrast, they would have been amazed when Jesus stopped to talk to someone as apparently unimportant as a poor, sick woman excluded from society and even her own family. It's easy to think that it's the 'upfront' people in church who are most valuable in God's eyes. But this story shows that's not so. It isn't always the leaders God values most. The long-standing church member sitting at the back, praying down God's power over the congregation, is of inestimable value in heaven.

■ PRAYER

Please, Lord, keep reminding me that praying is the most important thing I can ever do. Amen

Luke 7:6–7, 9 (NIV)

Faith

The centurion sent friends to say to him: 'Lord, don't trouble yourself, for I do not deserve to have you come under my roof... But say the word, and my servant will be healed'... When Jesus heard this, he was amazed at him, and turning to the crowd following him, he said, 'I tell you, I have not found such great faith even in Israel.'

We've been looking at some of the amazing things Jesus did for the people of Capernaum, and the love he showed them. After living so close to Jesus, wouldn't you think the entire village must have believed in him? Sadly, Jesus concluded that a foreigner displayed more faith than most of the locals. It was in the very synagogue built by this same Roman centurion that Jesus suffered such frequent rejection. But the doubting hearts of the people of Capernaum would cost them dear (Luke 10:15).

Do doubts about God's love, or power to take care of you, ever bother you? They attack most of us, particularly during tough times. I try to flick them away like flies on my forehead, rather than 'opening my mouth' to chew on them. I remember my mother always said, 'The God who taught me to trust in his name would not have brought me this far to put me to shame.'

■ **PRAYER**

Lord, help me to treat my neighbours like you treated yours and not as they treated you. Amen

Hungry for hope

Paul Harris

What is hope? It can be an emotion, an attitude, a positive frame of mind or a spiritual reality.

Hope is something I do (verb) and something that I have (noun). Hope comes in different forms. Realistic hope is based on experience and on promises kept. Unrealistic hope is little more than wishful thinking – the sort that invites the response, 'Dream on!'

When our editor invited me to write about hope, she was unaware that my dog is called Hope. She is a boisterous cockapoo (the dog, not the editor!), and we bought and named her after coming through a challenging couple of years that included serious illness, premature retirement and an enforced move. We felt tested to our limits. Eventually, we saw that God had been our safety net even when we thought we were falling. He was still our hope.

Most mornings, I walk along the beach calling out 'Hope'. I am controlling our dog and declaring a truth.

Nowadays, politicians make extraordinary promises and young people call everything 'awesome'. Perhaps, like me, you are tired of hype but still hungry for hope. I hope you enjoy this exploration of hope in the Bible.

1 Peter 3:15 (NIV)

Hope that intrigues

But in your hearts revere Christ as Lord. Always be prepared to give an answer to everyone who asks you to give the reason for the hope that you have. But do this with gentleness and respect.

My sense of smell is not as sharp as it used to be. Consequently, I fear I may use too much seasoning in my cooking and be too heavy-handed when applying aftershave. One Christmas, when I was still a vicar, one of the family bought me an aftershave called Pagan Man as a joke. I felt embarrassed when a parishioner noticed it and asked me what it was. I was tempted to say I had forgotten.

But hope should be a distinctive mark of a Christian, something people notice about us, like a scent that they find intriguing. Peter wrote from the bitter memory of having been unprepared in his younger days to admit that he was a friend and follower of Jesus. Forgiven and restored, he went on to face hardship, persecution and death. Writing in later life, he encouraged his readers to be ready to explain why it was they had an extraordinary, distinctive hope. This hope is a gift from God, which we should not be embarrassed to explain.

■ **PRAYER**

Lord of all hopefulness, help me this day to live a life that intrigues others, full of hope that I can explain and share with those who cross my path. Amen

Hebrews 6:18–19 (NIV)

Hope that secures

God did this so that… we who have fled to take hold of the hope set before us may be greatly encouraged. We have this hope as an anchor for the soul, firm and secure.

I served in two churches in Southampton, a port city with a rich maritime heritage. When choosing hymns or worship songs, anything that included sea imagery went down well. The words 'Will your anchor hold in the storms of life?' and the more recent 'All through the storm your love is the anchor, my hope is in you alone' are prime examples.

Anchors come in various forms. Their purpose is to keep the vessel secure in a storm or to stop it drifting on the tide. They are used most commonly when the ship is at sea, not when it is secured to the quayside, which is a lesson in itself.

This verse from Hebrews reminds us that Christians are all refugees who have fled and cling to the anchor of God's love.

But for an anchor to work, it must be attached. God's love is the unbreakable link that gives us hope.

■ **PRAYER**

Lord Jesus, you stilled the storm and gave peace to your disciples. I pray for those who feel overwhelmed or adrift. Be their anchor, and keep them secure in your love. Amen

Genesis 18:10–12 (NIV)

Ridiculous hope

[The Lord] said, 'I will surely return to you about this time next year, and Sarah your wife will have a son'... Abraham and Sarah were already very old, and Sarah was past the age of childbearing. So Sarah laughed to herself as she thought, 'After I am worn out and my lord is old, will I now have this pleasure?'

When I was young, I thought romance ended at 40. Growing older, it was a relief to discover this was not so. Romance, companionship and physical presence remain important.

Abraham and Sarah had been together many years. The pain of childlessness had been particularly hard for Sarah to bear. God had promised Abraham that he would create a special race through his descendants. Abraham was 100 and Sarah was 90, so they had long given up hope of having children. God surprised them by promising they would conceive in the conventional way. This seemed especially ridiculous to Sarah. She was told off for laughing like a giggly girl.

God's promises give us hope, but can seem ridiculous. As the angel told Mary when announcing that she would conceive Jesus, 'Nothing is impossible for God' (Luke 1:37, CEB). My parenting days may be over, but I am always open to new adventures with God.

■ PRAYER

Eternal God, keep wild hope alive in me, that I may still dream big dreams; ones that make you smile and others laugh, for your glory. Amen

Psalm 25:1–3 (NIV)

Hope that protects

In you, Lord my God, I put my trust. I trust in you; do not let me be put to shame, nor let my enemies triumph over me. No one who hopes in you will ever be put to shame, but shame will come on those who are treacherous without cause.

I wonder if you have a treasure box tucked away somewhere, full of mementos? I dig mine out from time to time. There are some surprising inclusions. What possessed me to keep my school reports? Nowadays teachers are bound to be kinder, or at least more careful in what they write. My reports include some acerbic comments that bring back moments of shame all these years later.

David the psalmist knew success and failure. He was gifted and chosen by God, yet he also acted shamefully. He had enemies throughout his life who gloated over his failings. Somehow, he held on to the hope that God would protect him from lasting shame.

The late Charles L. Allen once said, 'When you say a situation or a person is hopeless, you are slamming the door in the face of God.' Whatever others may have said about you in the past, God does not give up on you or condemn you to shame.

■ **PRAYER**

Lord Jesus, thank you for the hope that protects us from shame. Encourage those who feel bad about themselves. Amen

Jeremiah 29:11–12 (NIV)

Hope that encourages

'For I know the plans I have for you,' declares the Lord, 'plans to prosper you and not to harm you, plans to give you a hope and a future. Then you will call upon me and come and pray to me, and I will listen to you.'

This verse is very popular. Perhaps you have written these words in a card to encourage a friend facing uncertainty? I have received cards with them in when marking a milestone birthday.

Choosing cards is tricky; there is so much choice. There's a point in life when cards start to joke about age instead of congratulating you. I am not a fan of that. I think quietly to myself, 'Just you wait!'

There is a saying, 'You know you're getting old when your regrets outnumber your dreams.' Not very positive, if partly true. By contrast, the words from Jeremiah are encouraging because they are forward-looking and full of hope. They do not come with an age limit: 'Only suitable for the under-40s!'

There is no early retirement in God's kingdom. There are always new things to learn, and different ways of serving him. That encourages me, and makes me eager to know his good plan for my future.

■ PRAYER

Eternal Father, you are the God of the future. I pray for people young and old that I know who are facing uncertainty. Please encourage them with your promise of hope. Amen

Zechariah 9:9, 12 (NIV)

Hope that captivates

Rejoice greatly, Daughter Zion! Shout, Daughter Jerusalem! See, your king comes to you, righteous and victorious, lowly and riding on a donkey, on a colt, the foal of a donkey… Return to your fortress, you prisoners of hope; even now I announce that I will restore twice as much to you.

Words from this reading were used when Jesus rode into Jerusalem and have been repeated on every Palm Sunday since. Jesus' kingdom message included a declaration that prisoners would be released. The expression 'prisoners of hope' is not widely used, but appeals to me and stands out in this reading. Plays and films are sometimes described as 'captivating'. They draw us in by their beauty, their power or their plot. We want to know how the story ends.

God's hope can take us prisoner. He is a fortress or strong tower, our place of refuge. His hope is beautiful, not least because it was bought for us through the dramatic events of Jesus' death and resurrection. We can be confident we know how our own personal story and the greater story of the world will end. We are, inescapably, prisoners of hope.

■ **PRAYER**

Heavenly Father, be close to all prisoners today. Release me from any fear, resentments or guilt that hold me captive and make me instead a prisoner of your glorious hope. Amen

Romans 8:23–25 (NIV)

Hope that saves

We ourselves, who have the firstfruits of the Spirit, groan inwardly as we wait eagerly for our adoption to sonship, the redemption of our bodies. For in this hope we were saved. But hope that is seen is no hope at all. Who hopes for what they already have? But if we hope for what we do not yet have, we wait for it patiently.

The other day I was sitting in a hospital outpatient department waiting for an appointment – an all-too-frequent experience these days. Now, I am a great fan of health workers but I confess to reflecting ruefully that calling us 'patients' is a cruel irony. All too often I am well out of patience by the time I am seen. Bad for the blood pressure.

Bus stops also involve waiting. When I join the queue, there is no bus in sight. But the bus shelter, the timetable and the other waiting passengers all give me hope that eventually my bus will appear.

Paul used the word 'groaning' in a passage about waiting and hoping. He encouraged his readers, and us, to look ahead patiently for the day of redemption, when we finally receive the full benefits of having been saved and adopted as God's children.

■ PRAYER
Almighty God, help those of us who are not good at waiting and find ourselves getting impatient. Please give me the patience that I cannot find within myself. Amen

Colossians 1:25–27 (NIV)

Mysterious hope

I have become [the church's] servant by the commission God gave me to present to you the word of God in its fullness – the mystery that has been kept hidden for ages and generations, but is now disclosed to the Lord's people. To them God has chosen to make known among the Gentiles the glorious riches of this mystery, which is Christ in you, the hope of glory.

People sometimes speak of having been educated at the University of Life or in the School of Hard Knocks. Life can be wonderful, but also tough. Everyone has challenges and disappointments to deal with. Events and other people can leave us feeling bruised, hurt and fragile. The challenge lies in how we choose to respond. Wounds can leave their mark, but if possible we should let our hopes, not our hurts, shape our future.

When Paul wrote to the Colossian Christians, he encouraged them by telling them they had been let in on a wonderful secret; a mystery had been revealed to them: Christ was in them. Despite any past difficulties or mistakes they had made, God had chosen them. He turned them from being a bunch of no-hopers into people who had a glorious, powerful hope.

■ **PRAYER**

Jesus, the Word of God, today I thank you for the women and men who first shared with me the mystery of your hope. Help me to pass on the baton of faith to the next generation. Amen

Romans 15:4, 13 (NIV)

Overflowing hope

Everything that was written in the past was written to teach us, so that through the endurance taught in the Scriptures and the encouragement they provide we might have hope... May the God of hope fill you with all joy and peace as you trust in him, so that you may overflow with hope by the power of the Holy Spirit.

For nearly ten years, austerity has been the main feature of the UK and world economies. Some of us still remember post-war rationing. By contrast, there is no shortage in God's kingdom. Paul did not hold back when asking God to bless his friends in Rome. He asked God to fill them to overflowing.

'Overflowing' can be a good or a bad word depending on the context. A bath left to overflow results in mess, damage and recriminations. An overflowing bowl or cup is a symbol of good things, of abundance and generosity.

Overflowing with hope does not mean that we become unbearably optimistic or wildly unrealistic. In an old Monty Python comedy sketch, two knights were duelling. When one had his arm cut off, he uttered the immortal line, 'It's only a flesh wound!' In contrast, Christians should reflect God, the ultimate realist and ultimate optimist.

■ **PRAYER**

Lord God, I pray for people who are feeling worn out and spiritually dry. Please renew them by your Holy Spirit so that they may overflow with joy, peace and hope for your glory. Amen

Revelation 21:3–4 (NIV)

Timeless hope

Look! God's dwelling place is now among the people, and he will dwell with them. They will be his people, and God himself will be with them and be their God. 'He will wipe every tear from their eyes. There will be no more death' or mourning or crying or pain, for the old order of things has passed away.

Recently I came across a simple aide-mémoire about God's hope: **H**old **O**n **P**ain **E**nds. That really appealed to me. I was surprised I had not seen it before – perhaps you have?

Much of the teaching about hope in the Bible is given in the context of Christians facing pain in its various forms. Pain is wearying. Like many people, I have a morning ritual that involves a cup of tea and some tablets. My morning dose includes a painkiller or two. I know if it is wet outside without opening the curtains, as my sportsman's knees are an accurate barometer.

God's promise of heaven described in Revelation 21 gives us hope. Knowing that one day there will be no more pain of any kind, a day when tears will be wiped away and when grief and death are gone, keeps me going.

■ PRAYER

Lord Jesus, please be close today to those who are struggling with mental, emotional or physical pain. Renew their strength, still their fears and enrich their days with the hope of heaven. Amen

The Gift of Years

 Debbie Thrower founded and leads The Gift of Years programme. She has pioneered the Anna Chaplaincy model, offering spiritual care to older people, and is widely involved in training and advocacy. Visit **thegiftofyears.org.uk** to find out more.

Debbie writes...

Welcome to the latest edition of our Bible reflections exploring themes related to being in our more 'mature' years.

A woman in her 80s once compared prayer to 'a country walk with a friend'. She's someone who has deliberately spent time getting to know God and now I hope these reflections will help each of us to get better acquainted with him, while sharing one another's company.

Time spent reflecting on what it means to grow older is time well spent. In *Shaping the Heart* (BRF, 2011), Pamela Evans says, 'Fix your attention on God,' not least because 'he is able to see beyond whatever is currently overwhelming us... Trusting obedience will enable us not only to keep going and to play our part in challenging times now, but also to grow into the people he created us to be – ready and equipped to play even more of a part in due course.'

Pamela is right. Sensing ourselves being shaped by God, made fit for purpose, will mean our perspective is enlarged and our enjoyment of the 'present moment' is transformed.

Best wishes

Debbie

Meet the writer: Paul Harris

Could you begin by telling us a little more about yourself and your story?

Where to begin? I was a reluctant vicar's son, the reluctance being mine not my father's. Later I became more grateful for my heritage and roots. Faith became personal and began to make a difference in my late teens. On leaving school, I served briefly as a police officer. Then I felt a strong sense that I was going to serve God as a missionary or minister. I was ordained in my late 20s. For 35 years I served primarily as an Anglican vicar and for five years I was the Mission and Evangelism Secretary for the Evangelical Alliance.

When I was 48, I was diagnosed with advanced kidney cancer. I lived to tell the tale but was advised to retire seven years later. That was hard to do. Was I being faithless? Two years later, I had a heart attack. That makes me sound decrepit. I'm not. I wasn't ready for my life to be a pity party, so I applied myself to writing. I love my life as a writer, the variety and the opportunities it brings.

You write in your introduction of coming through difficult times, and naming your puppy 'Hope'. Was that in celebration or defiance?

Good question. Celebration and faith rather than defiance, I think. My wife Cathy and I knew we had come through a fierce storm, not unscathed but still intact. It was a new season of hope.

We love the titles of some of your pieces, the ones in which you take an unusual, original angle: 'Ridiculous hope', 'Overflowing hope', 'Hope that intrigues', 'Hope that captivates'. Would it be true to say that your understanding of Christian hope, and your experience of that hope, was changed and deepened by the difficult experiences you've had?

Hope has always been important to me. When I became a Christian in my own right, I lost my fear of death. The hope of heaven is crucial. By nature, I am an optimist who likes to have Plan B in place. God is the ultimate idealist *and* the ultimate realist, so I think I am on safe ground.

In one of your pieces there's the sentence 'When I was still a vicar...' How did you cope with the loss of that role, and how did you become aware of your new vocation as a writer?

It was difficult. Even though I had a good understanding of grief it still hit me – both of us – hard. It wasn't so much the loss of my role but the shock of having to move and adjust again to revised life expectancy. Being a vicar wasn't where I derived my sense of worth or security, it was wider things. Grief comes in many forms – not simply missing what we have lost, but sadness about what we might reasonably expect to have experienced. Grief works forwards too. I struggled with a sense of being diminished in health but didn't feel ready for full retirement. The speed of it all made it worse.

In another of your reflections, you write, 'Pain is wearying.' How have you hung on to hope in the midst of pain?

Pain can sap you at every level. Leaving the church and the people we loved was awful. Worshipping was important for us – doing so not as an act of will but as an act of obedience. Even when I was hurting, reacting badly or making poor decisions, I knew deep down that I was loved by God. I was fortunate to have six months of excellent psychotherapy. That gave me the opportunity to understand better the wild mix of emotions I was feeling. Of course, the encouragement of loyal friends meant the world to us.

Meet Christine Whild

Christine Whild is a retired music teacher and climate change campaigner. At 85, she is the oldest member of Abingdon Carbon Cutters and we first met her when she sat on a panel at an event in Dorchester Abbey to discuss the church's fifth Mark of Mission: 'Safeguarding the integrity of creation and renewing the life of the earth.' She has six grandchildren and another one on the way, and two great-grandchildren.

Christine, tell us a little bit about yourself. Who is Christine Whild?

In midlife, having had three children, I went under the scheme for older women who had never managed to go to college and got my teaching career under way. I didn't take a degree until much, much later but I got onto the teaching ladder and they said to me they would employ me until they found someone better. But I was still in that job for 15 years, until I had to retire to look after my husband who had developed dementia. I looked after him for 20-odd years and it was during that time that I took two further steps. I first of all got my LRAM – a teaching qualification in piano. And then I decided to take an Open University course, which I managed to do while my husband was very poorly because I could be sitting in the same room as him, but still be a million miles away.

So when did you get concerned about climate change?

All this time, I hadn't really thought much about the environment, but I realised that it was about time that I made a few more friends and so I wanted to join a few things. Every now and again in Abingdon they have a 'clubs and societies day', and I went along and looked at the Carbon Cutters stall. They seemed a nice lot and I joined them. I said, 'Right, what are these books that you've got here?' So they said they're all about climate change and I took one of them. Well, I didn't go to sleep until I'd read it from cover to cover and that really was a terrible eye opener to me: the fact that we are destroying the planet.

And to what extent did your delight in your grandchildren fuel your concern for these issues?

Oh, very much so! Because they're the ones who are going to suffer. We older folk have caused so many of the problems by amassing so much stuff and travelling all over the world. I didn't do so much travelling, but I was of the generation that filled our houses with stuff, and now we're all thinking we wish we could get rid of it!

To what extent is your activism a reflection or outworking of your faith?

It's definitely inextricably linked with my faith. We had a morning on climate change at my local church, just across the road from where I've lived for over 40 years, not organised by me, but I was part of it. We used this prayer: 'Forgive us, Lord, for often exploiting your creation, for failing to rule with love and wisdom. Lord, help us to heal the damage we have done to your creation. Help us to protect the biodiversity of the earth.' And all the prayers were associated with this verse from Deuteronomy 10:14 (NIV): 'To the Lord your God belong the heavens, even the highest heavens, the earth and everything in it.'

What would you say to older people who might feel it's too late for them to do anything that will make a difference?

I can understand that they might feel like that, but I do believe it's important that we should all do the little we can do. It says in the Bible that God sees every sparrow that falls to the ground. And if you think how many millions and millions of sparrows there are in the world… and I think it's the same with this. Each tiny action is worth doing. Now it's obviously worth it if, as well as the tiny action locally, we also write to our MP, write to the prime minister, write to our supermarkets and make our points to them. Praise them for what they've done, like charging for plastic bags, but then point out something else you'd like them to do. I intend to go to the council and ask them to show me where my plastic goes, and what they do with it.

And is there anything to celebrate or is it all gloom and doom?

There is good news, you know! We are making progress and that's often not realised. China leads the world in wind power. Haiti's hospitals are all powered by solar power. I've got a list of 37 pieces of good news like this. They say that one person on their own can't make much difference, and governments won't make much difference, but communities might if they all pull together. So, in towns and rural communities all over the world, people are getting together and making an impact. There is some good news and we ourselves must be part of that good news by doing the small things we can to contribute to the larger good news all over the world.

You are

 Carla McCowen is a retired consultant paediatrician. She lives in Wensleydale with her husband Jeremy, and has written poetry on and off throughout her adult life. She published her first collection, *The Call of the Curlew*, in 2011, illustrating many of the poems herself. She has been a spiritual director for twelve years and enjoys singing with the Ripon Choral Society.

In the preface to her collection *The Call of the Curlew*, Carla writes:

My poems have mainly been inspired by the natural world: by the rhythm of the seasons, by trees and hills, flowers and colours, birds and animals. They have also been a means of exploring my developing perception of the divine and sacred, and of human relationships. My own experience of coming into contact with wild things has given me some of the most profound and privileged moments of my life: watching an otter play, meeting a snake on the path, seeing a kingfisher perched on a branch in the river, hearing the song of a nightingale in some deep wood, or the call of a curlew on the high moor – are all moments which I remember and treasure.

If something in you responds to [my] poem, the poem becomes yours. A poem is after all a means of communication, requiring both a writer and a reader for its purpose to be fulfilled.

We chose this particular poem from Carla's collection *The Call of the Curlew* because it touches on so many of our themes: hope, welcome and Jesus the good neighbour.

You are

You are the blush of pink
in new dawn sky, delicate tracery
black twigs on winter tree
you are plovers wheeling in a cloud
of black on white
snow-covered mountain tops
moss-green valley fields
you are each pebble on the beach
each shell; interwoven matrix
of creation.

You are he who walked barefoot
on the hot sand of the desert
lay on the cold stones
wrapped in a thin robe
met jealousy, deceit and fear
with human love,
violence with compassion.

You are my eyes, the lifting in my heart
when I look and see.
You are my reaching out
my ache, my hollow emptiness
my singing and my silence
my illumination and my dark.
You are my stream, my channel
through which love flows.
You are the eyes of those I love.

Carla McCowen (used with kind permission)

Memory's treasure

Albert Jewell

As we grow older, our memories are probably the faculty that we cherish most, and we tend to worry if we sense we are becoming more forgetful. Memories chart our passage through every aspect of our life, including our spiritual journey. There will be happy memories, from which we derive continuing joy and comfort, and, inevitably, there will be unhappy memories too. These may fade over time but we can learn from them, and grow as people because of them.

Memories belong to groups as well as individuals. 'Do you remember when…?' we ask one another. Families, organisations and communities share memories: joyful, sad and testing experiences which strengthen the bonds between members. This is supremely so for the people of God. Throughout their scriptures, Jews are reminded never to forget how their God delivered them from slavery in Egypt, and in the New Testament, at his last supper on earth, Jesus told his disciples to 'do this in remembrance of me'. 'Remembering' in this context did not just mean casting their minds back, but rather re-experiencing what had happened, in the present.
And as we shall see, the same can be true for us 2,000 years later.

Deuteronomy 16:11–12 (GNB)

Slaves in Egypt

Be joyful in the Lord's presence, together with your children, your servants, and the Levites, foreigners, orphans, and widows who live in your towns. Do this at the one place of worship. Be sure that you obey these commands; do not forget that you were slaves in Egypt.

But of course they did forget, lamenting the long years of suffering in the wilderness rather than praising God for his deliverance. Are we as forgetful of what God has done for us?

When we say our prayers, whether in worship with others or on our own, it's good to begin by remembering the good things that we have experienced in recent days – however small they might seem – and to thank God for them.

But so that our praying is not just focused on ourselves, it's also good to remember that the Jews were commanded not only to recall their former slavery, but to use the memory of their suffering to inspire them to care for others less fortunate than themselves: the widows and orphans, the strangers and outcasts. Remembering what God has done for us should inspire us to remember others who are in need.

■ PRAYER

Father, forgive me that I can be so forgetful of your many blessings. Today I am especially thankful for… Help me to become more of a blessing to others by pointing me to someone in particular who may need my care and prayer. Amen

Numbers 11:4–6 (GNB)

Moaners all

The Israelites themselves began to complain: 'If only we could have some meat! In Egypt we used to eat all the fish we wanted, and it cost us nothing. Remember the cucumbers, the watermelons, the leeks, the onions, and the garlic we had? But now our strength is gone. There is nothing at all to eat – nothing but this manna day after day!'

The only thing I cannot eat without bad indigestion is cucumber. Not that I am particularly fond of watermelons, leeks and garlic either. I would, I think, have been quite content with the water, quails and manna God provided for his people in the wilderness. Indeed, the manna, described as a sort of sweet, honeyed cereal, sounds rather delicious. But the people in this Bible story moaned, forgetting that they had been slaves in Egypt, and moaning tends to be catching.

It's a pity if we only give thanks to God for providing for our basic needs at harvest time. But if we say the Lord's Prayer attentively, reminding ourselves that we are dependent on him for 'our daily bread', it's impossible to forget. And it's not 'my' bread we pray for, but 'our' bread. If we have enough, we can be truly grateful. If we have more, then it is for us to share.

■ PRAYER
Lord, when other people go without even the basics of life, help me to do all I can to put this right. Amen

Luke 17:32–33 (GNB)

Remember Lot's wife

Remember Lot's wife! Those who try to save their own life will lose it; those who lose their life will save it.

I wonder what your earliest memory is. I still remember, when I was about two and a half, and out on a walk with my parents, lying down in the road a few yards from home because I didn't want to go any further. To my horror, they took no notice and left me where I lay. It was a shocking lesson for a toddler to learn, but one I never forgot.

Jesus told his listeners to 'remember Lot's wife', who, we're told in Genesis, met a calcified end after disobeying the angels' instructions not to look back when fleeing from the destruction of Sodom and Gomorrah. This story would have been among the earliest in the communal memory of the Jewish people. By referring to it, Jesus was warning his listeners not to hanker after past comforts, but to be prepared for the new reality he was ushering in.

So, what is your earliest memory, and what do you learn from it?

■ **PRAYER**

Father God, reassure me that my life has been worthwhile in your sight, whatever mistakes I have made. Forgive me when I have failed to learn from past mistakes, and help me to know that you are always at my side as I walk with you into the future. Amen

Exodus 20:8, 11 (NRSV)

Holy day

Remember the sabbath day, and keep it holy... The Lord blessed the sabbath day and consecrated it.

Not being brought up in a Christian churchgoing family, I used to find Sunday rather boring, except in summer when I could watch or play cricket. But when I went to church during my university years, Sundays became the most important day of my week. Our Christian fellowship groups led a service in a country chapel each term. We prepared well, and all took part and enjoyed a lavish farmhouse tea afterwards.

Little has changed more in our lifetimes than the typical Sunday: most shops are now open, many people have to work, children have lots of weekend activities and far fewer people go to church.

Enshrined in the Old Testament is the importance of keeping one day in the week holy, or special for God, and for rest, renewal and remembering. For Christians that day is Sunday, because that is when Christ rose from the dead.

What are your memories of past Sundays? What was good about them; what was bad? Has Sunday changed for better or worse in more recent years? Can you find ways to 'remember the sabbath' even if your routines have changed over the years?

■ PRAYER

Father God, this special time of resting in your presence is very precious. As I open myself to your Spirit in prayer, may I find your renewal in the depths of my being. Amen

Psalm 88:12–13 (NRSV)

The forgetful land

Are your wonders known in the darkness, or your saving help in the land of forgetfulness? But I, O Lord, cry out to you; in the morning my prayer comes before you.

When I retired from full-time ministry I thought I would no longer need to memorise the names of all the people in my churches. A big mistake! I've met so many new people since I retired, and I struggle to remember their names.

The good news is that even though we may forget so much – and even forget God – God never forgets us. He holds us in the hollow of his loving hand. He remembers our name. If you are suffering from memory loss or caring for someone with dementia, it's vital to hold on to that assurance. As the priest and neuropsychologist Joanna Collicutt writes, 'There is nowhere beyond the reach of God in Christ, and no state so low or ambiguous it cannot be raised up by his transforming power.'*

■ **PRAYER**

Father God, whatever shadowy valley I find myself in, please hold my hand. Give me patience and understanding for myself, and as I meet those who feel that they are living in the land of forgetfulness. May I hold their hand, even as you hold mine. Amen

* Joanna Collicutt, *Thinking of You: A resource for the spiritual care of people with dementia* (BRF, 2017).

Mark 8:17–18 (NRSV)

Don't you remember?

Jesus said to them, 'Why are you talking about having no bread?
Do you still not perceive or understand? Are your hearts hardened?
Do you have eyes, and fail to see? Do you have ears, and fail to hear?
And do you not remember?'

Jesus often sounds frustrated that his close disciples seem to miss the point of what he says and does. He challenges their perception and their memory. Faced with a large crowd who were getting hungry, he is amazed that the disciples have already forgotten what happened last time they were in that situation.

I have not infrequently felt like those disciples. I can be 'a bit slow' in my relationship with Jesus. Why, if he has helped me in the past when I faced a challenge, do I find it so difficult to believe that he will do the same in the present and the future? Why do I not remember?

When was the last time you felt God had helped you in difficult circumstances? When have you been most aware of his presence? Can you allow those memories to reassure and sustain you in whatever you are facing now and in the future?

■ **PRAYER**

Lord, I remember how you have heard and answered my prayers, and how you have stayed close to me. Give me the confidence to know that you will always hear my prayers, and walk beside me, all the way to my journey's end. Amen

Luke 22:19–20 (NIV)

Remembering Jesus

And he took bread, gave thanks and broke it, and gave it to them, saying, 'This is my body given for you; do this in remembrance of me.' In the same way, after the supper he took the cup, saying, 'This cup is the new covenant in my blood, which is poured out for you.'

As Jesus faced the imminent end of his earthly life, he shared a last poignant meal with his disciples. They must have wondered what he meant by saying that the bread they ate was his body and the wine they drank his blood. Even more mysteriously, he told them to remember him and his sacrifice whenever they ate together in future.

Most churches seek to honour Jesus' command through a regular service, whether it's called Holy Communion, the Lord's Supper or the Eucharist. This is one of the main ways in which Christ's memory has been kept alive among his people, and, as I said in my introduction to this series, 'remembrance' in this context doesn't mean casting our minds back, but rather experiencing Jesus as present with us in the here and now.

Reflect again on what Holy Communion means to you. How else do you experience Jesus present with you in your life today?

■ PRAYER

Lord God, Holy Communion is a glorious mystery. At one level it is simple: we take the bread and drink the wine as Jesus told us to do. The mystery lies in the way in which we can take him into our inmost beings, and in this we rejoice. Amen

Luke 23:39–40, 42 (NIV)

Lord, remember me

One of the criminals who hung there hurled insults at him… But the other criminal rebuked him… Then he said, 'Jesus, remember me when you come into your kingdom.'

Does God have a memory? The prophets and psalmists of old certainly thought so, as they petitioned him to remember his past mercies and not to remember their past sins. Maybe such things concern us more as we grow older.

Professor John Swinton of Aberdeen University won the 2016 Michael Ramsey Prize for outstanding theological writing, for his book *Dementia: Living in the memories of God* (William B. Eerdmans, 2012). He comes to the conclusion that 'as long as God remembers us, who we are will survive'.

As we grow older, we may worry about what happens after death, and whether we will be remembered. Of course we will be remembered for a while, by our families and friends and all those who have known us. But for how long, we may wonder? John Swinton's words give great reassurance, not just for those with dementia and their loved ones, but for all of us who face the diminishments that age can bring. As long as God remembers us, who we are will survive, and God's memory is eternal.

■ PRAYER

Lord God, Jesus shows us that you are ever-loving and ever-forgiving. Help us to find peace in the knowledge that, through him, we shall live on in your memory for ever. Amen

Hebrews 13:1–3 (GNB)

Practical remembering

Keep on loving one another as Christians. Remember to welcome strangers in your homes. There were some who did that and welcomed angels without knowing it. Remember those who are in prison, as though you were in prison with them. Remember those who are suffering, as though you were suffering as they are.

In my early ministry, which was mostly among young people, I greatly enjoyed sharing hospitality with students who were away from home. I learned so much and we entertained some lovely human angels.

Those to whom the author of Hebrews was writing may have been good at caring for their Christian friends, but needed reminding of their wider responsibilities: to strangers, those in prison, the sick and suffering. I loved hearing about the elderly congregation in the Hebrides who were the first to offer accommodation and support to a Muslim refugee family. And in my own city of Leeds, it's mostly older people who volunteer in a scheme offering a night or two's bed and breakfast to a young person who would otherwise be on the street.

Remembering those in need – the sick, the poor, the stranger, the prisoner – is not just noticing them; it is doing something practical to help them. What thing – however small – can you do today?

■ PRAYER

Heavenly Father, you are my refuge and strength and provide for all my needs. Help me to remember the needs of others, and show me what I can do to help those in need. Amen

1 Corinthians 11:1–2 (NIV)

Remembering others

Follow my example, as I follow the example of Christ. I praise you for remembering me in everything and for holding to the traditions just as I passed them on to you.

As I reflect on the course of my life and on my spiritual journey, I have become increasingly grateful for those who have influenced me for good. My father, although an atheist, rightly insisted that one's reason is a most important gift and must be used well. I am grateful to the minister, now long dead, who brought me to Christ. I am grateful to the many young people whose questioning and verve have been wonderfully challenging. And to so many others…

Whenever Paul wrote to his churches, he found things to be thankful for in them.

I wonder, who have been the most important examples for you in your life? Who have been your spiritual mentors? Are they all in the past or are some more recent? Have you been able to tell them and thank them for their influence on your life? And if they are no longer alive, could you thank God for them as you remember them today?

■ **PRAYER**

Heavenly Father, I thank you for so many people who have helped me in life. Help me in my turn to be a good example to my family and neighbours so that something of Christ may be visible to them, in me, to your greater glory. Amen

Made to feel welcome

Ro Willoughby

When my children were small, we lived on a college campus. Students would often come to our home, for formal meetings and for social occasions. One day I heard the doorbell ring. My four-year-old son opened the door before I could get there. I heard him say, 'Come in. Can I take your coat? And would you like a drink?' I was highly amused. He spoke in exactly the same way that I did, although he was far too young to fulfil his offer of a cup of tea or coffee.

In these reflections we are focusing on how God welcomes us, particularly looking at the way Jesus welcomed everyone. The idea of feasting with God occurs several times. Because we know we are welcomed by him, we can delight in knowing he has accepted us.

But the Bible also tells us that we too should be 'welcomers', continually inviting God into our lives. The Holman Hunt painting *The Light of the World* portrays Jesus so clearly in this role, as he knocks on the door, waiting for someone on the other side to let him in.

As you read these reflections, may you experience God's warm invitation to come to him on a daily basis.
And may you, in your turn, assure him that he
can find a home with you.

Mark 1:16–18 (NIV)

Jesus' invitation

As Jesus walked beside the Sea of Galilee, he saw Simon and his brother Andrew casting a net into the lake, for they were fishermen. 'Come, follow me,' Jesus said, 'and I will send you out to fish for people.' At once they left their nets and followed him.

Just occasionally someone offers me an invitation I simply cannot refuse – to make use of a friend's holiday cottage, or the gift of a dress ordered by my sister (which didn't fit her but she knew it would suit me). By accepting, I am acknowledging my appreciation not only of the gift but also of the giver.

Simon and Andrew had already been introduced to Jesus. So when he met them while they were fishing, they knew enough about him to accept his invitation, drop their nets and go with him. They could hardly have known what it meant to 'fish for people'.

Jesus goes on welcoming us to follow him. What do you know about Jesus that means that you would want to spend time with him?

■ PRAYER

Lord Jesus, thank you that you always welcome me to spend time with you. I know that you are someone who is caring, strong and... [add your own words]. Amen

Luke 14:16–18, 21 (NIV)

Welcome guests

Jesus replied: 'A certain man was preparing a great banquet and invited many guests… He sent his servant to tell those who had been invited, "Come, for everything is now ready." But they all began to make excuses… Then the owner of the house became angry and ordered his servant, "Go out quickly into the streets and alleys of the town and bring in the poor, the crippled, the blind and the lame."'

If we are invited to a wedding or special celebration, we must have a good reason not to accept. To think, 'I'm too busy' or, 'I just don't want to go' may be honest but is not a good enough reason to refuse. The host in Jesus' story was determined that every seat at his table would be filled. He was prepared to invite people who are not usually invited to anything special.

Jesus invites all people, however rich or poor, important or insignificant, old or young, to come to the feast in his kingdom. If people refuse the invitation, there are plenty of others who will accept.

Imagine yourself eating a special meal with Jesus. What a treat! How welcome do you feel?

■ PRAYER

Lord Jesus, thank you that you welcome everyone to feast with you, old and young, well and sick, all races and cultures, rich and poor… and that includes me! Amen

Luke 18:15–16 (NIV)

All children welcome

People were also bringing babies to Jesus for him to place his hands on them. When the disciples saw this, they rebuked them. But Jesus called the children to him and said, 'Let the little children come to me, and do not hinder them, for the kingdom of God belongs to such as these.'

There is something very touching about the scene in the Gospels where parents bring their helpless babies to Jesus. He already had a reputation for caring for the vulnerable, needy and unnoticed in society. It used to be said that children should be seen and not heard. This was clearly how Jesus' disciples treated these children.

But that was not how Jesus viewed them. In strong language, we are told that he was cross with his disciples and went out of his way to welcome the babies. Not only did children matter to him, they were also a pattern for how we all come to God, in simple trust.

Picture this story and be glad that Jesus does not turn anyone away who wants to come to him.

■ PRAYER

Jesus loves me, this I know,
For the Bible tells me so.
Little ones to him belong,
They are weak but he is strong.*
Amen

* Anna Bartlett Warner (1827–1915)

Luke 4:40–41 (NIV)

Jesus welcomes the sick

At sunset, the people brought to Jesus all who had various kinds of illness, and laying his hands on each one, he healed them. Moreover, demons came out of many people, shouting, 'You are the Son of God!' But he rebuked them and would not allow them to speak, because they knew he was the Messiah.

As the sun sank in the sky, those who had been at work all day had time to bring to Jesus their friends and relatives who were sick or whose minds were disturbed. He touched them, as evidence that he accepted them. And he healed them all.

We can imagine the joy that resulted from this. 'Who is this Jesus?' they would have asked. But he was not ready yet for people to know that he was God and had come from God. It was enough that they knew they were welcomed by this man who had the power to heal.

However much or however little we know about Jesus, one of the most important things to know is that he loves us.

■ **PRAYER**

Lord Jesus, thank you that you love me, more than I can ever imagine. As the sun sets this evening, remind me just how much you love me. Amen

Matthew 11:28–30 (NIV)

Walking together

Come to me, all you who are weary and burdened, and I will give you rest. Take my yoke upon you and learn from me, for I am gentle and humble in heart, and you will find rest for your souls. For my yoke is easy and my burden is light.

A few months ago I was sitting in a marketplace café in a North Yorkshire town. A small boy got himself worked up into a paddy. For the next 20 minutes, I watched the father as he got down on his knees to speak to his son face-to-face. For a while, they then sat side by side on the wall of a memorial stone. Eventually, the father led his son across the square, walking hand in hand. This father was giving all the time his son needed, not telling him off, just being there for him.

Jesus invites us to walk with him, to let him comfort and strengthen us. But walking with him means we go in the direction he takes us. We share his yoke. We acknowledge he is Lord. There is no better place to be.

■ **PRAYER**

Lord Jesus, thank you that I am always welcome to walk with you wherever you want to take me. As I walk hand in hand with you, may I find rest and strength. Amen

Isaiah 55:1–3 (NIV)

Welcome if you're thirsty

Come, all you who are thirsty, come to the waters; and you who have no money, come, buy and eat! Come, buy wine and milk without money and without cost… Listen, listen to me, and eat what is good, and you will delight in the richest of fare. Give ear and come to me; listen, that you may live.

A few years ago, various celebrities were given a supermarket shopping trolley and ten minutes to fill it with whatever they wanted. This resulted in a mad dash to pile as much as possible of the more expensive food into the trolley.

God's invitation here is less frantic and more lasting. He bids his people to come to him to quench their thirst – water, wine and milk are available. What's more – it's all free. And there's free food on offer too, the richest and most delicious available. Most people enjoy a feast even if our appetites might shrink as we get older.

This is not really about food and drink. This is the offer of a life lived consciously in God's presence, life 'to the full' (John 10:10), a life of contentment and peace whatever our circumstances. This is God's offer to each one of us.

■ PRAYER

Lord God, you have invited me to your feast, to sit with you and enjoy the food you provide. Please help me to accept your invitation and be at peace, sitting with you at your table. Amen

Psalm 23:5–6 (NIV)

Welcome to God's home

You prepare a table before me in the presence of my enemies. You anoint my head with oil; my cup overflows. Surely your goodness and love will follow me all the days of my life, and I will dwell in the house of the Lord for ever.

We have just moved house. It has been lovely to invite people to visit us to look around our new home. God does not have a home as such, for he is not restricted to any one place.

Nonetheless, the Bible contains many references to God's house, his holy temple and even to his desire to make his home with us. God welcomes us into his territory with an invitation to come to his place, to share it with him and to feast with him at his table, protected from danger and fear. It comes with the promise of goodness and mercy surrounding us, knowing we can be God's 'housemate' for ever.

Wherever you live now has become God's home, because he is there with you. Welcome him afresh into your home and your life.

■ **PRAYER**

As I look around the room I am now in, may I know for certain, Lord God, that this is your place, for you have made your home with me. Amen

James 4:7–8 (NIV)

Welcoming God

Submit yourselves, then, to God… Come near to God and he will come near to you. Wash your hands, you sinners, and purify your hearts, you double-minded.

There is usually more than one way of looking at something. In this series, we have explored how God invites and accepts us into a relationship with him. But another way to think about our theme is to reflect on the ways in which we welcome God.

The Holy Spirit has been given to every believer to empower them to live holy lives. But every follower of Jesus has to play their part too. That's why James challenged his readers to acknowledge God, to come close to him, to make an effort. In response, God himself will come close to them.

I spend a lot of time with children in schools and in church. I often challenge parents to do all they can to help their children discover how much God loves them, so that in response the children will want to love God. It's a two-way process. God loves us, so we love him. We come close to him, so he comes close to us.

■ **PRAYER**

Run the straight race thro' God's good grace,
Lift up thine eyes, and seek his face;
Life with its way before us lies,
Christ is the path, and Christ the prize.*
Amen

* John S.B. Monsell (1811–75)

Psalm 24:3, 7–8 (NIV)

Fling wide the gates

Who may ascend the mountain of the Lord? Who may stand in his holy place?… Lift up your heads, you gates; be lifted up, you ancient doors, that the King of glory may come in. Who is this King of glory? The Lord strong and mighty, the Lord mighty in battle.

The city of Jerusalem, built on the mountain known as Zion, was where the temple had been constructed. This was where people came to worship God. It was God's holy place, as this psalm, probably written by King David, says: God lived there.

The gold-covered ark of the covenant, containing the stone tablets on which were inscribed the ten commandments, was also seen as a symbol of the presence of God. The ark travelled around with God's people. But it was captured by their enemies, the Philistines. Eventually, King David brought it back to Jerusalem with much singing and celebration. The 'ancient doors' were to be flung open to welcome the ark into the city. Of course, Jesus himself rode into the city of Jerusalem on a donkey. The crowds welcomed him – for a short while.

God is already in his city, but he also has to be welcomed into the city. In the same way, God is already with us but we also need to continue to welcome him.

■ **PRAYER**
Lord God, may I fling wide the gates to let you into my life this day. Come, Lord God, come! Amen

Revelation 3:20 (NIV)

Open the door

Here I am! I stand at the door and knock. If anyone hears my voice and opens the door, I will come in and eat with that person, and they with me.

I love it when, after a long journey, I ring my daughter's front doorbell. Almost always she is standing close to the door and immediately she throws it open, hugs me and is clearly delighted to welcome me. In contrast, it's a truly horrible feeling if someone is expecting me but they're clearly not pleased to see me when they open the door.

This verse from Revelation inspired Holman Hunt's famous *Light of the World* painting, with its three versions: one on display in Christ Church, Oxford, one in Manchester and the largest in St Paul's Cathedral, London. Jesus is pictured waiting outside a door which only has a handle on the inside. Is anyone going to open it? Will they be pleased to do so?

Each day, Jesus waits for us to welcome him, from the inside, to whatever we are doing and wherever we are going. Whoever opens the door opens the way for Jesus to come in to feast with them.

■ PRAYER

Lord Jesus, today I am throwing open the door of my life to welcome you. 'Come on in!' Thank you that you wait so patiently for me to respond, for you long to be with me. Amen

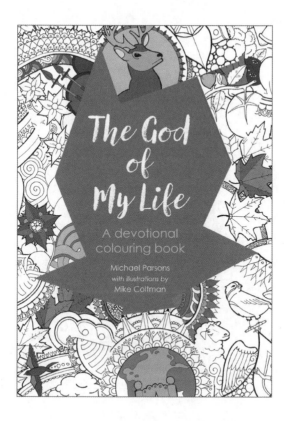

Doodling and colouring help many of us to be present in the moment, giving us more focus and aiding concentration. This unique book offers a whole-psalm reference for each design, with specific verses highlighted and brief devotional comments and questions to help the reader to reflect on scripture, their own lives and their relationship with God while colouring in.

The God of My Life
A devotional colouring book
Michael Parsons
978 0 85746 584 9 £8.99
brfonline.org.uk

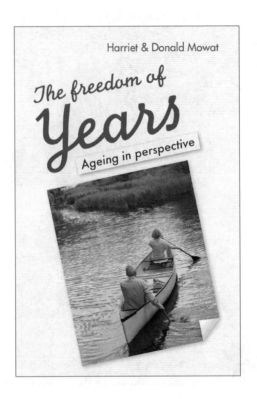

Harriet & Donald Mowat

The freedom of

Years

Ageing in perspective

This positive, affirming book explores and reviews the meaning and purpose of our lives. As Christians, ageing gives us the opportunity to deepen and even transform our spiritual lives. *The Freedom of Years* helps those who want to undertake the journey by examining the ageing task, the inevitable changes and the possibilities of joy along the way. Read this book, see the potential and seek to age in the light of your Christian faith.

The Freedom of Years
Ageing in perspective
Harriet and Donald Mowat
978 0 85746 506 1 £10.99
brfonline.org.uk

In this unique book, Wanda Nash reflects on growing old with faith
and a positive spirit. This compelling invitation to grow old boldly
– full of her own experiences and insights – includes the author's
reflection on her encounter later in life with terminal cancer, and her
thoughts on coping with the daily challenges of living a Christian life
in her illness and in ageing. Wanda's indomitable spirit is matched
only by her fresh vision of the love of God in Jesus Christ.

Come, Let Us Age!
An invitation to grow old boldly
Wanda Nash
978 0 85746 558 0 £6.99
brfonline.org.uk

To order

Online: **brfonline.org.uk**
Telephone: +44 (0)1865 319700
Mon–Fri 9.15–17.30
Post: complete this form and send to the address below

Delivery times within the UK are normally 15 working days. Prices are correct at the time of going to press but may change without prior notice.

Title	Issue*	Price	Qty	Total
The God of My Life		£8.99		
The Freedom of Years		£10.99		
Come, Let Us Age!		£6.99		
Bible Reflections for Older People (single copy)	May/Sep* 18	£4.99		
Bible Reflections for Older People (10–24 copies)	May/Sep* 18	£4.75		
Bible Reflections for Older People (25–49 copies)	May/Sep* 18	£4.50		
Bible Reflections for Older People (50 or more copies)	May/Sep* 18	£3.99		

delete as appropriate

POSTAGE AND PACKING CHARGES			
Order value	UK	Europe	Rest of world
Under £7.00	£2.00	£5.00	£7.00
£7.00–£29.99	£3.00	£9.00	£15.00
£30.00 and over	FREE	£9.00 + 15% of order value	£15.00 + 20% of order value

Total value of books	
Postage and packing	
Total for this order	

Please complete in BLOCK CAPITALS

Title .... First name/initials .... Surname................

Address ....

.... Postcode ....

Acc. No. .... Telephone ....

Email ....

Method of payment

☐ Cheque (made payable to BRF) ☐ MasterCard / Visa

Card no. ☐☐☐☐ ☐☐☐☐ ☐☐☐☐ ☐☐☐☐

Valid from [M][M] [Y][Y] Expires [M][M] [Y][Y] Security code* ☐☐☐

Last 3 digits on the reverse of the card

Signature* .... Date .... / .... / ....

*ESSENTIAL IN ORDER TO PROCESS YOUR ORDER

Please return this form to:

BRF, 15 The Chambers, Vineyard, Abingdon OX14 3FE | enquiries@brf.org.uk
To read our terms and conditions, please visit **brfonline.org.uk/terms**.

The Bible Reading Fellowship (BRF) is a Registered Charity (233280)